Leading with Cheese, Fish, and Carrots

The Propaganda of Team Leadership:

How Leadership Euphemisms Demoralize and Destroy Teams

by Martina Sprague

Copyright 2013 Martina Sprague

All rights reserved. No part of this text may be reproduced in any form or by any means, electronic or otherwise, without the prior written permission of the author.

Acknowledgements:

Front cover image pictures Emmentaler Switzerland PDO Cheese. Image source: Dominik Hundhammer, reproduced under Wikimedia Commons license.

Back cover image pictures simple mouse in search of cheese. Image source: Seans Potato Business, reproduced under Wikimedia Commons license.

TABLE OF CONTENTS

Introduction	4
We Would Rather Be Ruined Than Changed	8
One Man's Treasure Is Another Man's Trash	16
Goals Under Construction	21
Winning Hearts and Minds	28
Passing the Buck	32
Jack and Jill Went Up the Hill	36
A Matter of Timing	40
Gone Fishing (but not at the *Fish!* Market in Seattle)	48
Those Pesky Four-Letter Words	52
The Empty Suit	59
Cosmic Clause Vision	66
Notes	74

INTRODUCTION

Having read hundreds of books about leadership, I have grown tired of trite sayings attempting to define it on a bumper sticker: "You manage things but lead people." Okay, so what? To lead means to take somebody somewhere. Okay, this is obvious. What else is obvious? It is obvious that the leader cannot exist without the followers. The opposite is not necessarily true. The followers can benefit from the leader's direction and wisdom, but they do not need him or her in order to exist. Understanding this relationship between leader and follower places the role of the leader in the proper perspective.

The leader's first responsibility when attempting to express a vision, solve a problem, reach a consensus, and lead the team toward the goal is to define reality; to think critically, encourage response, and avoid getting trapped in meaningless sayings. Chinese statesman and military leader Deng Xiaoping (1904-1997 CE) informed us that debate tends to make things "complicated."[1] He was right, of course, but likely had only his own interests in mind. The fact that your followers do not accept an atmosphere of strict obedience should be celebrated. If you can draw strength from their resourcefulness, you will welcome doubt without viewing it as an assault on your person. In fact, a healthy dose of talk and debate can have the effect of bringing down barriers, not raising them.

At its core leadership is about understanding human nature. Adolf Hitler (1889-1945 CE), in *Mein Kampf*, spoke about the "small measure of thinking power the broad masses possess,"[2] thereby reminding us that understanding human nature is also an essential key to controlling it. Cringe if you will at my use of a quote from he who is perhaps the most despised man in modern history. But being clever, even insightful, is not synonymous with having an admirable character. Hitler was right. Had the masses utilized their thinking power properly, there is a good chance that the Holocaust would not have happened. He also said, "I found it difficult to understand how men who always had reasonable ideas when they spoke as individuals with one another suddenly lost this reasonableness the moment they acted in the mass."[3] It is called groupthink in modern lingo, and tends to occur within a group of people who are trying to reach a consensus without applying critical thought and analysis. Joseph Goebbels (1897-1945 CE), Hitler's minister of propaganda, understood that any mantra repeated often enough is apt to become viewed as true. Thus without a proper understanding of human nature, ranting about how there is no "I" in team and together everybody achieves more could have dangerous consequences. The dissenters, those who question your ideas, may be your most valuable employees because they counteract this groupthink mentality and help you achieve a more balanced perspective.

This book is not so much about leadership per se, as it is about how to think about leadership by learning to ask the appropriate questions and learning to find the appropriate answers. It explores the strengths and weaknesses of leadership propaganda, motivational sayings, and groupthink. The material in this book is excerpted from the previously published book, *Leadership, It Ain't Rocket Science: A Critical Analysis of Moving with the Cheese and Other Motivational Leadership Bullshit*, also by Martina Sprague.

> "Of the best rulers, the people (only) know they exist."
>
> — Lao-tzu

> "Few are those who can see with their own eyes and hear with their own hearts."
>
> — Albert Einstein

> "The brightest flashes in the world of thought are incomplete, until they have been proved to have their counterparts in the world of fact."
>
> — John Tyndall

WE WOULD RATHER BE RUINED THAN CHANGED

Does leadership have a goal? The purpose of leadership studies is inevitably to achieve victory. The leader can wear different hats. He can lead from the front or the rear; he can present the team with charismatic speeches or follow a model based on Maslow's Hierarchy of Needs. Individual goals further influence how he or she views and writes about the discipline. Proponents of different leadership theories have attempted to inspire current and future leaders without understanding that it is really the followers and not the leaders who need inspiration, because they alone decide whether or not they will follow. Furthermore, much of what has been written about leadership is noncritical. Although it includes statistics and fancies, it excludes deeper examination and analysis. We accept as presented what we find in books and manuals even as we have no idea to what extent or if it is founded upon sound principles. This leaves us at a crossroads without a standard to guide us. To move a step closer to understanding the relationship between leader and follower, we will examine, compare, and contrast the tools managers and leaders commonly use when trying to implement new ideas by appealing to the passionate side of the workforce.

When I read Marcus Buckingham's and Curt Coffman's book, *First, Break All the Rules: What the World's Greatest Managers Do Differently*, I thought it the soundest book about leadership ever written. However, I am sorry to report that I cannot say the same for various other "cookbooks" for leadership, ranging from *Who Moved My Cheese? An Amazing Way to Deal with Change in Your Work and in Your Life* by Spencer Johnson and Kenneth Blanchard to *Fish! A Remarkable Way to Boost Morale and Improve Results* by Stephen C. Lundin, et al. Amazing? Hardly. Remarkable? I don't think so. How do we know?

Leadership books and seminars commonly open with anecdotal stories for engrossing the listener. Anecdotes and parables can be viewed as the cornerstones for further discussion. A graphic example is *Fish!* which opening paragraph portrays the typical Monday morning attitude: "It was a wet, cold, dark, dreary, dismal Monday in Seattle. . ." Despite the depressing weather and having suffered the recent death of her husband, Mary Jane, the protagonist of the story, has a reputation as a "can do" supervisor. In sharp contrast to Mary Jane's work ethics, however, the "large operations group on the third floor" has become an "unresponsive, unpleasant wasteland." When Mary Jane accepts a promotion to manager, she suddenly sees the "light" and realizes that "we choose our attitude."[4] Wow! What a revelation! (I'm being facetious, of course.) The trick and, subsequently, the gist of the story is how to teach this insight to the "unpleasant wasteland" on the third floor.

Another graphic example is *Who Moved My Cheese?* which provides a parable portraying two mice in search of cheese. (Cheese, in this case, symbolizes that which one treasures, normally one's current job because it is also one's livelihood.) The purpose of the story is to demonstrate how to deal with unwanted change by "moving with the cheese," or not letting the loss of your job (and your livelihood) dictate how you feel about your future. "But, have you noticed how we don't want to change when things change?"[5] asks one character in the story, thus setting the pace for the inevitable change that will follow. It is suggested that rather than stewing about the loss of your job, you should pick up your virtual running shoes and chase after new "cheese" (a new career). By doing so you acknowledge that how you ultimately deal with change has nothing to do with external factors, such as corporate greed or an economic depression, but can be boiled down to your attitude which is the root of all your problems. In my view, adopting a positive attitude is a superficial and overly simplistic solution to dealing with change. Real problems, such as the loss of one's job and livelihood, require real solutions and not just a "good attitude."

However, a reason why these sorts of books are so popular, or even needed, is because the authors realize that employees naturally resist change, and that management will face a barrier every time they are the carriers of bad news such as job cuts, pay cuts, or reorganization where employees are negatively affected and forced into new positions or new duties. But good leadership, although a complex issue, ain't rocket science, and the reliance on anecdotes and metaphors for success can backfire by making the readers of such books feel underappreciated, or worse, insulted and manipulated as evidenced by the volume of less than flattering reviews on Amazon.com for *Fish!* and particularly for *Who Moved My Cheese?*

What do these reviews say? A few examples include "corporate brainwashing" for managers who believe in change for change's sake; and patronizing, shallow, and insulting to the reader's intelligence. The message of *Who Moved My Cheese?* is that "you must not struggle" and must "accept change without regard to whether it is appropriate or not," says one reviewer. The book is clearly written for those with power to be presented to those without power. "It is little wonder that managers, CEOs, teachers, and pretty much anyone with authority over others praise this book," says another reviewer and suggests that the book is "used as a tool by management to cow their herds into submission." The ancient Greek historian Thucydides reminded us that the natural law of humanity is that the weaker are subject to the stronger, and those who are stronger can naturally use their strength to force their subjects into compliance. Thus the strong do what they can and the weak suffer what they must. The "moral of the story," says one reviewer, "is that we should not get angry when our life bread is constantly moved and hidden from us by some invisible higher power. Instead, we should not only embrace the fact [that] we are being messed with, but also have FUN with it."

Although it may appear as though I am unfairly picking on this particular book, the reason why is because it turned out to be such a tremendous bestseller and thus a book that many of the readers will likely be familiar with. To be fair, it should be mentioned that the book has received just as many positive reviews, but the number of one-star reviews at nearly five hundred is still overwhelming and sends a clear message about how employees come to distrust management when they feel they are being manipulated.

Who Moved My Cheese? can thus be used as a tool by management in lieu of direct communication when major and unpleasant changes in the form of layoffs and pay cuts are on the horizon. I am not alone in this assessment. Barbara Ehrenreich, social critic, journalist, and author of *Bright-Sided: How the Relentless Promotion of Positive Thinking Has Undermined America*, notes how "the promoters of positive thinking present those with a negative attitude, even when it comes to lay-offs and deep pay cuts, as 'whiners.'"[6] She goes on to say:

> The motivation industry could not repair this new reality. All it could do was offer to change how one thought about it, insisting that corporate restructuring was an exhilaratingly progressive "change" to be embraced, that job loss presented an opportunity for self-transformation, that a new batch of "winners" would emerge from the turmoil. And this is what corporations were paying the motivation industry to do. As the *Washington Post* reported in a 1994 article on motivational products, "Large corporations are looking for innovative and cheap ways to boost employees demoralized by massive layoffs." [In the 1990s], AT&T sent its San Francisco staff to a big-tent motivational event called "Success

1994" on the same day the company announced that it would lay off fifteen thousand workers in the coming two years.[7]

The two mice in *Who Moved My Cheese?* try to keep life simple by avoiding analysis and debate. (Remember that debate tends to make things complicated, as suggested by Chinese statesman and military leader Deng Xiaoping.) This is a classic example of what is wrong with seeing the glass as half-full rather than half-empty for fear of being called a whiner. Change, management suggests, is merely a steppingstone to success, and a layoff is really just an opportunity to start that new career you always wanted, no matter the fact that you will not be able to pay your mortgage or feed your family while you are scurrying around in the labyrinth in search of new cheese. In my view, a better approach, as Ehrenreich points out, is to "acquire the skills not of positive thinking but of critical thinking, and critical thinking is inherently skeptical. The best students—and in good colleges, also the most successful—are the ones who raise sharp questions, even at the risk of making a professor momentarily uncomfortable."[8]

Who Moved My Cheese? will no doubt prove suitable for leaders discussing with other leaders what leadership ought to be, but with no interest in involving the subordinates in the decision-making process. Moreover, success through positive thinking has limits. Although the adage, "Move with the cheese!" might reinforce what one already believes, it will unlikely have lasting value or cause an about-face with respect to a situation that has already gone bad. A good leader must commit himself or herself to studying leadership with a critical eye. Here the authors fail to think the thought to conclusion; they fail to ask the appropriate questions and fail to restate the problem from the perspective of the opposition in a way that is satisfactory to the readership. Believing that you can teach people to like change, or stop "hemming and hawing" and "just move with the cheese," suggests either careless or arrogant thinking.

Implementing drastic change when faced with a global economic depression is one thing. But some leaders, supervisors, or managers try to implement change even when change is not needed and the system ain't broke to begin with. Why? Sometimes it is to further their own interests. They know that if they can present a list of "improvements" to their managers or the company, they have a greater chance of being promoted. They can then leave their current position for some higher assignment elsewhere and leave the disgruntled employees to deal with these "improvements" that were not welcome to begin with and did not create greater efficiency. Employees are more willing to change when they recognize that there is an advantage to changing. Before asking people to change, the intelligent and critical leader makes an absolutely honest assessment of his or her true reason for desiring change, and asks if the change will truly bring improvement. He must also be willing to live the change. If his sole motivation is a promotion, the fact that he is dishonest will quickly come to light and sabotage the respect his employees have previously afforded him.

In contrast to *Who Moved My Cheese?* Marcus Buckingham's and Curt Coffman's book,

First, Break All the Rules, offers several realistic insights about employee motivation and efficiency at work. Rather than trying to plant the "good vs. bad attitude" idea in the minds of employees who complain about change, the authors suggest that you should accept people as they are by recognizing that people have feelings and are naturally resistant to change. The best you can do is avoid generalizations and "[f]ocus on each person's strengths and manage around his weaknesses."[9] In other words, if you have to announce job or pay cuts, accept the fact that your announcement will be received with a great deal of negativity. Then solicit ideas from employees that may make the change less painful and, whenever possible, avoid forcing people into positions they are not interested in. "We would rather be ruined than changed, we would rather die in our dread than climb the cross of the moment and let our illusions die," said British-born American poet Wystan Hugh Auden (1907-1973 CE).[10]

ONE MAN'S TREASURE IS ANOTHER MAN'S TRASH

Fish! in my view, is not quite as disturbing as *Who Moved My Cheese?* However, the ideas presented in the book are likewise missing good follow-through. Although there is no doubt that choosing your attitude and having fun at work can provide employees with the capacity to create a more enjoyable work environment and, therefore, more productivity and better relations with customers, the book assumes that we agree on the definition of fun. Yet I can hear the grumbling at my job if the manager were to interrupt in the middle of coffee break (as suggested in the book) and make it mandatory for everyone to cancel whatever plans they might have for lunch and go to the fish market, because "it is so much fun." The issue has now shifted from, "Let me show you something really fun," to "I am in charge here and decide how you should spend your lunch break." As a result the manager has already alienated at least some of his or her workforce.

If you desire to know your people better, is the fish market necessarily the best place to accomplish this? Perhaps you should invite them to dinner, to your home, on a camping trip, or to a ball game? Any of these ideas may prove satisfactory, but they may also prove disastrous. Furthermore, what should you do with those on your team who do not want to go to whatever outing or activity you have planned? It is, after all, not for you to say whether or not your employees will enjoy spending time with you. Some people enjoy their own company better, or that of their family for that matter. Believe it or not but some people would rather stay at work and work a normal day than spend time in the company of their boss at some picnic or other "fun" event. As an example, one company recently organized a "tour" of sorts in a different city, which purpose it was to show appreciation for the workforce, reinforce the importance of customer service, and promote teamwork by making the employees partake in "friendly" competition. The initial memo that was issued with respect to this idea stated that it was "mandatory" for employees to attend the event, even though it would require spending a night away from home in a shared hotel room with a stranger. When enough people had grumbled, the company thought better of it and made participation voluntary.

When an employee refuses to take part in your suggestions for fun, it does not mean that he or she is inherently a bad worker without social skills, nor does it mean that he or she is not a team player. Although choosing one's attitude and making an attempt to have fun as professed in *Fish!* might indeed create an enjoyable work environment, more productivity, and better customer relations, the same can be said for running a tight ship. When trying to implement new ideas that foster a fun atmosphere at work, you should also not forget to ask what the customer thinks. Say Marcus Buckingham and Curt Coffman about customer service in the airline industry:

> [A]irlines forget that customers don't usually choose one airline over another by comparing safety records. Whatever the airline, customers fully expect that

they will arrive at their destination unharmed. They demand safety, but they are not impressed by it. It is the wrong outcome for airlines to emphasize. Southwest Airlines again stands out as the exception. Their flight attendants are experts in all the required safety procedures, but safety is not the point of their work. Fun is the point.[11]

I applaud the authors for their deep insights into successful leadership, but must confess that I disagree on this particular point. To know whether or not the authors are correct, one must first ask the customers who fly Southwest Airlines what they think. It is possible that some customers would find Southwest's leadership model disturbing and would rather have a quiet experience onboard that allows them to read a book or work on their laptop undisturbed. Again, the point is that people's ideas of fun differ. One man's treasure is another man's trash even when it comes to fun. The lesson is: Do not assume. Whether you are dealing with your employees at work or with the customers, make an effort to ask how they really feel. And remember that it is not for you to decide what another person should think is fun.

What tricks in addition to those described previously do companies and motivational writers and speakers use when attempting to motivate employees through the adoption of a "good attitude" and "fun" activities? At one company in briefing one day, the leadership came up with the not so brilliant idea that employees should do a self-evaluation to create peer pressure that would motivate them to work harder and more efficiently, on the premise that work has more meaning when there is a bit of friendly competition involved. If you accomplished a lot in one day you would rate yourself highly on the score card, and if you accomplished a little you would give yourself a lower score. The score cards would then be displayed daily on the bulletin board for all to see. One worker with an outstanding work record raised his hand and asked, "What if we don't want to participate in this exercise?" The leadership answered, "Then you can go home!" Rather than making an effort to learn why this worker was not interested in participating, the leadership punished him merely for asking a question. If you were to take an educated guess, to what extent do you think the leadership managed to motivate this employee?

Here is what happened: After the briefing, the employee went to the leadership's office and expressed dislike for the treatment he had received. He was then somehow suckered into developing the score cards for the exercise. He spent a whole evening at home working on this project without compensation. But when he returned the next day with the score cards, the idea never went into effect. Why? Because by then it had become obvious to the leadership that adults will not play games they have no interest in playing. "When you come up with a bullshit program, you will get bullshit results," the employees told the leadership. But rather than admitting that forcing people to compete who have no interest in competing will not increase their motivation, the leadership said that they had never intended to implement the idea in the first place, but wanted only to find out who would approach it with a good attitude and who wouldn't.

If you are in a leadership position and you have an idea for a new program and your people tell you that it won't work, will you listen to them? Or will you tell them that their attitude sucks? Or perhaps you will use the common excuse that one cannot know whether or not an idea will work before one has tried it? Common sense should tell you differently. Do you like liver? No? Good, I don't either! And, you know, even if I had never tried it, I still wouldn't have the desire to eat it just to find out if I were correct in my assessment of my taste buds. Past experiences along with gut feeling will give a good indication of how efficient a new program or idea is even before one has tried it. Moreover, people are not inherently lazy. Most of us want to work and enjoy contributing with our ideas to increase the efficiency of our organization. Still, what motivates you may be a turnoff to me and vice versa. Thus whether or not games and friendly competition are good motivators is not immediately clear. Motivational ideas cannot be taken at face value just because they are stated in a book that has hit the bestseller list.

GOALS UNDER CONSTRUCTION

Rather than accepting the fact that one man's treasure can be another man's trash, we often try to fit everybody under the same umbrella especially when it comes to motivational ideas. But you cannot change the fact that the world is made up of all kinds of personality types simply because you think you have found this great new way of "transforming" people. As we have seen in the previous examples, when management suggests that employees should split into teams and compete for the Holy Grail at the end of the rainbow, the suggestion might backfire because many people are not competitive and therefore not motivated by the idea of competition no matter what the prize. Having fun at work by playing games will only appeal to some of the workers. To take this a step further, consider suggesting to a highly efficient employee that he or she should apply for a supervisor position because "he is so talented," or because "he would be great in the job," or because "people like him need to use their fullest potential," or because "he is wasting his time and talent in his current position." If you are surprised when he refuses your suggestion, it may be because you don't understand that everybody does not value the same things or the same ideas.

Despite its somewhat corny title, Adrian Gostick's and Chester Elton's book, *The Carrot Principle: How the Best Managers Use Recognition to Engage Their Employees, Retain Talent, and Drive Performance*, rises above *Fish!* and *Who Moved My Cheese?* with respect to changing employee attitudes, by emphasizing that "[w]hile leaders cannot often change the tasks in their organization, they can change employees' attitudes toward their jobs by setting clear corporate goals," and "[a] good share of an employee's attitude toward work is internally driven by a person's desire for autonomy and achievement."[12]

According to Gostick and Elton, "In business, a carrot is something used to inspire and motivate an employee."[13] If the employee's goal does not coincide with management's goal, or if you have a problem with the current accomplishments of your team, it is better to say so straight out and talk about what can be done (in other words, to call a spade a spade) rather than beating around the bush with sublime messages that act as turnoffs to the greater part of the workforce. Face it: Some people work for you only because they need to put food on the table and not because they feel any particular allegiance to your company. If we force people to set goals, many employees will set goals that they have not thought much about rather than goals that lead to something of true value.

Cookbook approaches to leadership, such as *The One-Minute Manager* by Kenneth H. Blanchard and Spencer Johnson, or *The 21 Indispensible Qualities of a Leader* by John C. Maxwell, tend to tempt leaders to fall in step with yet another graphic example of a new, efficient, and creative way of doing business. Leaders constantly get trapped in meaningless ideas and sayings that they shamelessly pass on to their followers, sometimes because they proudly believe that it is everybody's responsibility to smile, be proactive, work smarter and not harder, and, above all, that there is no "I" in team, and other times because they know how little thinking power the masses possess. More often, these sorts of leadership approaches offer little new insight. In fact, some of the slogans are so obvious that to mention them in polite company would seem arrogant: "Talent is a Gift, but Character is a Choice."[14] Okay, so what? Not to discuss them, on the other hand, comes with the risk of causing discourse and reality to diverge on separate paths.

Although hundreds of people have offered advice on leadership and leaders are generally fond of using acronyms and analogies when trying to motivate their employees, the phrases and slogans they use are highly imprecise and often rely on what one thinks sounds good at the moment without basing it on factual research. The same ideas and slogans are rehashed over and over without considering their deeper meaning, and are often merely repeats of what other leaders have said or happened to hear at some seminar they attended long ago. In any practical sense, they do not go beyond that first fuzzy feel-good moment and do not explore what happens next. It is also not uncommon for workers who are exposed to these slogans to avoid questioning their validity, and as a result feel unhappy and dissatisfied with their place of employment when the sayings don't deliver what they promise. To gain proper understanding as an employee you must sometimes be prepared to take the opposite stand and have the moral courage NOT to be politically correct; the courage to dissent openly when management tells you that it is everybody's responsibility and there is no "I" in team. It takes guts to stand up and tell a superior exactly whose responsibility it is (perhaps the janitor's when it comes to cleaning the break room). It takes guts to stand up and tell a superior that he is wrong when suggesting that there is no "I" in team, because the individual—yes "I"—is, in fact, the most important part of a successfully run team.

But how do you know if an idea is valid or not? Consider the following example: You are a motivational speaker teaching a class for supervisors. You tell your audience to clasp their hands and note which thumb overlaps the other. Then you tell them to release their hands and clasp them again. Does the same thumb overlap this time? (Hint: It will for just about everybody.) You now tell your audience that the reason why is because "we have a bad attitude that makes us reluctant to change." The problem with this explanation is that simply holding a demonstration and making a statement does not make it so. What if one person in the audience has the moral courage to speak up and tell you that the reason why the same thumb overlaps the other every time you clasp your hands has more to do with muscle memory and whether you are right or left-handed than with a bad attitude that makes you resistant to change? If you give a right-handed person a pen and asks him or her to write their name on a piece of paper, then ask them to put the pen down, then ask them to pick it up and write their name again, you will find that if they used their right hand the first time they will use it also the second time. You are not going to make a right-handed person more efficient at writing by forcing him or her to use the left hand.

Now let's say that you are a somewhat smarter motivational speaker trying to teach your group about change. First you ask everybody to change something in their clothing, such as undoing a necktie, placing their wristwatch on the other arm, or taking a shoe off. Once they have complied, you ask them again to change something in their clothing. Again, they comply. Now, for the third time, you ask that everybody change something in their clothing, but you give no reason for the change. By now you can hear grumbling in the audience. They are beginning to distrust you (the leader). You will now tell the audience that the point of this exercise is to demonstrate that when employees cannot see the benefit of change, they are reluctant to change. You will explain that success is reached by convincing the employees that the change will be beneficial to them. This is pure logic: To convince a person to agree with a conclusion, you must first convince him or her to agree with the premises. If he or she does not agree with the premises, the conclusion will never follow. Yes, you can force change, but if you do your team will not respect you as a leader, they will not stand behind you. You will lose your most important asset: your people. Is it worth it? It has been said that great leaders venture out and find challenges. But keep in mind that the leader cannot exist without the followers and many followers are not interested in challenges that will upset their daily routine. This should be obvious but somehow seems to escape us.

A successful change in attitude must thus be accompanied by clearly defined real change. When sitting in traffic frustrated with the gridlock, rather than thinking of the stop-lights as "go-lights" (as some motivational speakers have suggested), one might opt for leaving home five minutes earlier, choosing an alternate route or, if possible, changing work hours. If you intend to lead with cheese, fish, and carrots, you might want to acknowledge that anecdotal stories and slogans rely on personal conviction rather than hard evidence. Moreover, a person's attitude toward work is largely driven by internal ambitions, and carrot type motivators work only in limited circumstances. According to Daniel H. Pink, author and speechwriter for former Vice President Al Gore:

> For enduring motivation, the science shows, a different approach is more effective. This approach draws not on our biological drive or our reward-and-punishment drive, but on what we might think of as our third drive: Our innate need to direct our own lives, to learn and create new things, and to do better by ourselves and our world.[15]

People are far more likely to change their attitude about a project if they have some ownership of the idea. Ownership is not related to how much money you make, what types of fringe benefits you get, or what kind of uniform you wear. Can you give one specific example of how your team feels ownership? If you were to ask this same question of your team, would they respond with the same example? A way to test if your ideas have value is to restate them from the perspective of the employees. Is it possible that you believe your team feels ownership of an idea, but when you ask them about it they won't know what you are talking about? As reinforced in

The Carrot Principle, one of the strongest indicators of employee satisfaction is an opportunity for the employee to do what he or she does best every day.[16]

WINNING HEARTS AND MINDS

Why do we go to work each day? Our jobs are important to us, so important in fact that we go to work even when we hate our jobs. We need the income, but we are also evaluated as people in conjunction with our occupations. What is the first question you ask a new acquaintance? Where do you work? Or, what do you do for a living? Some factors are particularly important in determining how happy we are at work, including permission to decide the specific methods by which we do our job or complete a task. If you have the opportunity to do the things you are good at and enjoy, you will be more likely to come to work with a good attitude, excel, be productive, look for solutions to problems, and less likely to take excessive sick days. This should be obvious. Thus barriers are not necessarily broken by cross-utilizing employees and forcing them to work in areas where they don't want to work. This sort of behavior is more likely to cause discontent, lack of productivity, and more sick days.

Furthermore, how big a part your employees can play in problem solving and how secure they feel at work is directly related to how much information they receive. A common reason for negative reactions toward change is that people feel secure in their present positions and like things "the way they are." Another reason is lack of information about the change. Nobody likes coming to work only to discover that their "map" no longer matches their surroundings. Change should not be implemented solely for the sake of change; however, there are many reasons why a good manager might want to implement change in the workplace. For example, he or she may want to increase the efficiency and quality of the organization and product; new requirements from customers might make change necessary; or some of the current tasks may prove unprofitable and outdated. Something has to be done, but what?

Change can take many directions and a solution that works well for one company may not work equally well for another under similar circumstances. Conceptually, however, there are certain stages of change that can act as guidelines and make your employees feel that their opinions count:

1. **Planning.** This involves selecting representatives from the different departments that the change will affect, who will then brainstorm for the best way to implement the change. When brainstorming, the task is not to come up with as many suggestions as possible, but to come up with the fewest number of truly good suggestions.

2. **Mapping.** Problems can be targeted and diagnosed through discussions in small groups or one-on-one between management and employees. A list of issues to be discussed will keep the session on track. Remember to talk about both good and bad points; things that already function well and things that need to be remedied. Otherwise the positive things that don't need change may be overlooked in the strife for change, and the end result may be change for the sake of change but without really making things "better."

3. Implementation. Before a change can be implemented, it must be considered in view of the ideas that emerged during discussion and brainstorming sessions. During the implementation stage of the change, those affected must get the full support of management, and management must be open to further suggestions for fine-tuning the change.

4. Evaluation. An honest evaluation a few weeks and again a few months after the change has been implemented will help guard against employee and customer dissatisfaction. If the change did not accomplish the desired results, more fine-tuning is needed with employee input openly talked about and valued.

Thus before implementing new ideas the leader must first win the hearts and minds of his people. Successful leadership requires insight into human personality, which cannot be summarized in a simple saying posted on your office door. No matter how great the idea is, unless others feel ownership they are not likely to support you. Just ask yourself whose ideas you like most: those that you come up with yourself or those that somebody else comes up with? Generally we like our own idea best regardless of whether or not it is really the best idea. Even though it is difficult to achieve your best by keeping things the same, you must consider how change affects others. Employees will more readily accept change if the idea originates with them and not with the supervisor or manager. If the leader wants his people to accept change, he must be ready to listen to and implement changes suggested by the employees.

PASSING THE BUCK

But what if one of your employees suggests a change that you agree with, but you must push it past the higher managers in the chain of command and get approval before you can implement it? Are you willing to do this? At one company, although the supervisor often said that he agreed with the workers, he still passed the buck: "I hear you and I agree, but management doesn't want us to do that!" Sometimes the team leader or boss tries to distance himself from the matter by transferring responsibility to the team through such jargon as, "it has come to my attention . . ." instead of "I have noticed . . ." or "safety is everybody's responsibility," instead of "I am responsible for your safety," or "to tell you the truth," instead of "I don't know but will find out," or the dreaded "you know what I mean?" which effectively bars all further questioning.

Going through the chain of command is often a terrible sacrifice of time and effort and your needs will likely get lost in the bureaucracy. A chain also tends to break at its weakest link. If the chain breaks, you will get no further than to the broken link.

> There was only one catch and that was Catch-22, which specified that a concern for one's own safety in the face of dangers that were real and immediate was the process of a rational mind. Orr was crazy and could be grounded. All he had to do was ask; and as soon as he did, he would no

longer be crazy and would have to fly more missions. Orr would be crazy to fly more missions and sane if he didn't, but if he was sane he had to fly them. If he flew them he was crazy and didn't have to; but if he didn't want to he was sane and had to.[17]

The Catch-22 is that to get anything done you must go through the chain of command, because only the top has the authority to do something. But the closer you are to the bottom, the less important the matter seems to the top. Those who can do something about the matter have the least interest in doing anything. But to get anything done, you must enlist the people who are the least interested in doing something.

Some leeway with principles will always work to your benefit. Managers who try to lead the employees from behind a desk in an office located at headquarters many miles away will make faulty assumptions. Things can look great in theory or on the drawing board, but when you enter the trenches, events will not come down exactly the way you thought. After all, your employees do have brains. Even worse is to preach one thing and do another. When you set contradictory rules from behind a desk, as soon as you leave the office and enter the real world where things happen, you will discover that it is impossible to follow all rules as stated. You will therefore break some rules to "facilitate efficiency," or whatever statement you choose to justify your behavior. Your team will not view your behavior kindly unless you also extend the same flexibility to them.

Let's say that your employees complain about the work schedule and you recognize that ownership is important to motivation. So you tell them to delegate one person on the team as the "scheduling agent," who will be responsible for constructing a work schedule that everybody is reasonably happy with. You might have been against this idea at first but feel relieved on second thought, because now you have more free time on your hands which allows you to disappear to the coffee shop. When the work load suddenly gets heavy, the scheduling agent comes to you and complains that he doesn't have enough people to place on the schedule. You tell him, "Hey, you guys wanted to be in charge of scheduling. Deal with it!" This happened at my place of employment. Supervision took advantage of the fact that they were relieved from scheduling responsibilities. They hid in the coffee shop and generally took longer breaks, while the employees often worked without a break at all. There were days when I got one three-minute break all day, which I really couldn't afford, but I had to go to the bathroom some time!

This example may seem like a contradiction. First we complained that supervision made all the decisions. But when they gave us responsibility to decide, we complained that they did not do anything to help us. But there is a difference between being "bossy" and being a leader. If you delegate responsibility for a task that was previously yours, such as scheduling (even if the employees ask for it), it does not give you authority to hold out your hands and say, "Hey, you got what you wanted," when they complain. The leader must still be there for his team when they need him no matter what the situation. Passing the buck does not relieve you of responsibility. Passing the buck is like running over a bicyclist with your car and saying that it was not your fault that he died because he was not wearing a helmet! It is easy to pass the buck. Even worse is when it is done as openly and shamelessly as in the example described above.

JACK AND JILL WENT UP THE HILL

Now that you have had some time to let these ideas settle, the grand question is: Can human nature be changed, or is there even such a thing as human nature? Are we born to behave a certain way, or can our behavior be molded to fit a particular leadership model? The answer is that human nature cannot be changed because nature is by definition the inherent feature or characteristic of an organism, which in essence means that it cannot be changed. However, human behavior can be changed, but only at a considerable cost. If you do a risk/benefit analysis, you will most likely find that the price of change is often too great for the value. So if you cannot offer clever slogans and visits to the fish market to motivate people to change for the long haul, how do you know which leadership model to use and which leadership books have value? You start by doing a *Jack and Jill*.

Jack and Jill went up the hill . . . A very interesting law professor once taught me a most important leadership lesson that lies hidden in the first sentence of this simple nursery rhyme. Who are Jack and Jill? A boy and a girl, you say? How do you know? What if Jack is really Jacqueline? What if Jack is a jackass (a donkey)? How did Jack and Jill get up the hill? Did they walk, run, crawl, or bike? Did Jack carry Jill or did Jill carry Jack? How big is the hill? Is it a molehill or Mount Everest? Is the hill grassy, rocky, steep, or shallow? How long did it take Jack and Jill to get up the hill? Do the answers to these questions really matter?[18]

The value of an idea lies in the substance and not in the words. You must be specific and not general in your definition if you want your ideas to have meaning. To answer a question intelligently we need access to certain information about the central substance, or the gist of the thing discussed, which means that we must do a *Jack and Jill*, or ask pertinent questions for the purpose of defining the subject. In fact, on one of our exams in law class we were given a scenario and were graded on our ability to ask as many questions specifically pertaining to the scenario as possible, or to use a cliché: to leave no stone unturned. What I took from this is that our greatest pitfall is assumption: assuming that others think like you and like what you think; assuming that the right leadership or the right attitude can change people; assuming that we agree on what is right; assuming that bigger or more is better and smarter is better than harder; assuming that we agree on smarter; assuming that strength is in numbers; assuming that there is no "I" in team and together everybody achieves more; assuming that two heads think better than one, that there are no dumb questions, and that we should all move with the cheese; assuming that if it ain't broke there is still room for improvement; assuming that the customer is right; assuming that we all like to have fun and laughter is the best medicine; assuming that we agree on fun; assuming that proactive is better than reactive and today is the first day of the rest of your life; assuming that zero tolerance is productive or even possible; assuming that we all work toward the same goal; assuming that value-added, result-driven, quality-driven, and strategic fit have meaning; assuming that win-win is better than win-lose and half-full is better than half-empty; assuming that thinking outside the box is necessary and if nothing is ventured nothing is gained; assuming that the ballpark is safe; assuming that the ideas that empower you also empower others; assuming that people are responsive to empowerment or even know what it is; assuming that communication means exchanging verbal or written messages; assuming that it is everybody's responsibility; assuming that there really is a bottom line and that leaders are made, not born . . . Or is it the other way around?

It has been said that leadership mistakes made in the planning are the most difficult to forgive, because it often means that those affected are doomed before they even start. But since leadership theoreticians don't deal with the complex problems of life in the trenches, when reading leadership books whether for educational purposes or simply to pass time, how do you guard against stumbling into the wrong trench? You start by going a step beyond the obvious and taking possession of what you hear and see. The good leader comments and questions and speaks of what he or she knows from experience and gut feeling. The good leader seeks support from a team that is extraordinarily able and committed. The good leader does a *Jack and Jill* (a dissection of the meaning) on every problem and asks as many questions pertaining to the scenario as possible. The good leader acknowledges that being politically correct often blurs one's vision. The good leader challenges himself or herself to see things as they are and do what is right.

Defining the steps along the way is important

because definitions provide expectations of what the team will accomplish and open the door for questions and debate, which further aid the leader in fine-tuning the journey and help him avoid as many obstacles as possible. The leader who can restate a problem from the perspective of the opposition in a way that is satisfactory to *them* (not to the leader) can be reasonably assured that he has defined the problem and communicated it clearly. To take ownership of an idea, the leader must carry a thought to conclusion. Employees can likewise guard against manipulative practices conducted by the leadership by doing a *Jack and Jill*, or as has been said:

He who doesn't know and doesn't know that he doesn't know is an idiot.

He who doesn't know and knows that he doesn't know is uneducated.

He who knows and doesn't know that he knows is sleepy.

He who knows and knows that he knows is wise.

Let us move on and look at some situations you may experience as a team leader or team leader candidate. As we do so, think about how to ask the appropriate questions, how to leave no stone unturned; in short, how to do a *Jack and Jill* on every problem that comes your way.

A MATTER OF TIMING

Who becomes a leader? The leader is set apart from the rest; he is in his position because he has worked hard and is committed, and because he has certain qualities that will prove helpful to the workers and the company. At least this is the way it is supposed to be. But in reality it is the people who choose their leader regardless of his or her official title. You don't become a leader by placing a "supervisor" patch on your shirt; you become a leader by exercising certain qualities that make others want to follow you. When I asked one of my supervisors if he could find me a roll of tape, he grouchily waved his hand and said that I could go and pick it up in the supply room. When I asked a different supervisor the same question, he looked up from his desk, smiled, and said, "I have now taken on the role of supply clerk." Three minutes later he came back with the tape. Which of these supervisors do you think received the higher score on my unofficial leadership evaluation?

Now answer this question: How do you know that you are a team leader? Is it because it is in your job description? Is it because of that convincing little speech you held during your team leader interview? Is it because you have an outgoing personality and work well with others? Does your company require that you become a team leader before they allow you to climb to a higher position, because that is how the promotion chain works? Do you have to know how to lead people before you can manage things? Is leadership for everybody and can anybody learn it?

Or can you be a great manager even if you are a poor team leader and vice versa? (Are leaders born or made?)

Imagine this: You are a manager interviewing a team leader candidate, and ask her to tell you about the most challenging situation she has ever experienced and how she resolved it. She answers, "I have never faced a situation that was a real challenge." Based on her answer, how do you know whether or not she is fit to be a leader? How do you determine, based on her answer, whether she is inexperienced, cocky, or deals so well with challenge that nothing is difficult? Perhaps she just lives a dull life? Although a good leader should not be abrasive, she does not need to be overly friendly either. Outgoing can translate into gung-ho and annoying. For example, you might translate a team leader's constant radio chatter as "excellent communication skills," and her bossiness as "great team player." But does the team feel the same? If she is too enthusiastic, her team might find her dominant or flaky or plainly irritating, and so, her enthusiasm will not rub off on the team. Will you hire her? How do you decide?

When hiring for a job opening, there is normally an elimination process that may involve education, background, experience, etc., with certain minimum requirements. But how do you know, once you have weeded out certain people, that the core group you are left with is really those who will do the best job for you? If you use pre-employment tests, they should be relevant to the job. For example, some companies require applicants for jobs that are physical in nature to pass an agility test. But does an agility test really measure what is important? I would personally much rather work with those who are less strong but have motivation and work ethics, than with those who are more strong but lack a desire to work. It is almost impossible to rate efficiency based on physical characteristics and educational background. People excel when they have a passion for the job.

When determining where somebody fits, you might start by looking at recurring patterns in his or her performance. Even qualities that initially seem undesirable, such as not working well with others, interrupting others in conversation, being impatient, or demanding that all work be finished an hour early, are not by nature bad qualities. They become so only when we misunderstand how to use them, or when we try to eradicate or change them instead of making good use of them.

Thus whether the wheel that squeaks gets the grease or whether silence is golden is a matter of timing. Whether a quiet person is a good or bad communicator is a matter of timing. A quiet leader is not necessarily afraid of telling his team what he wants them to do. Success is relative. You want a successful person to be part of your leadership team, but what determines success in your particular company? Is success measured by how much money the leader makes for himself or the company? Is success measured by how the leader's superiors or subordinates view him or her? Is success measured in matters unrelated to the job; for example, marriage and family, background and education, or health and fitness? Whose opinion is more important? Why? An academic degree is not absolutely necessary for achieving excellence in leadership, but it is necessary to know how people learn, how to solve problems and, in general, what makes your team tick. So what does make your team tick? If in doubt, the simplest way to find out is by asking them! This should be obvious but often is not. Should the leader be committed to the company or to the team or to both? The obvious answer is probably to both, but if you *had* to make a choice?

Now define the qualities of a good leader. But remember, as you brainstorm, that there is a danger: Listing everything that comes to mind does not mean that everything has merit. When we say that something is "everybody's responsibility," we diminish the value of the responsibility. When we say that a leader should be good at thirty different things, we likewise diminish the value of each of these things. As an example, let's say that you have a problem with safety, so you call on your employees and ask that each comes up with three things that would provide a safer work environment. If you have one-hundred people working for you, you would potentially get three hundred answers. If you implemented them all, would you really achieve your objective of a safer work environment, or would you perhaps create a problem where there was none? Focus should be placed on identifying "real" safety issues and correcting them in a timely manner. But you must first identify the procedures that are actually causing a problem rather than helping it. Having too many procedures may in itself be a safety concern. Telling somebody what to do is easy; telling them how to do it is more difficult. Writing a long list of desired leadership qualities is easy; defining how it should be done is more difficult. To reach success with brainstorming, you need to discriminate.

So now, armed with a bit of background information about *Jack and Jill*, if you were to interview somebody for a team leader position, what questions would you ask? How do you picture the perfect team leader? What kinds of skills does he have? Be specific. Don't say good communication skills; rather say that he should hold a briefing once a day, listen to the concerns of the employees, and follow up the next day on questions or issues. The idea is not to come up with as many suggestions as possible, but to come up with the fewest number of good suggestions. When selecting a leader, this is your first opportunity to discriminate and narrow the list. For example, you might find the following attributes desirable leadership qualities:

1. A good leader is a team player.

2. A good leader identifies the objective and organizes a plan.

3. A good leader utilizes his team to reach the objective.

4. A good leader ensures that the team works with minimal friction toward the achievement of the goal.

Although this list is a good start, it fails to define the terms. What is team play? How does the leader go about identifying the objectives and organizing a plan? How does he motivate his team to reach the objectives, and how does he anticipate and minimize friction between team members? A team leader wants to be successful, but just exactly what is meant by the word success? Success to one person is not necessarily success to another. Each characteristic or issue should be defined and broken down into its component parts, until there is no question about its exact meaning. This exercise is a great confidence builder as well. Once you have defined every term for yourself, you can with confidence disagree with any issue that is discussed, because you know exactly where you stand and why and can thus argue from a position of strength.

Furthermore, in job interviews or interviews for promotions the interviewer has sometimes decided beforehand, based on personal opinion, whether or not the applicant will be awarded the job. The applicant's performance in the interview therefore carries little weight. In cases where the interviewer doesn't know the applicant beforehand, the first impression may decide the outcome. The questions and answers used in the interview will then merely help rationalize why this person should or should not be hired. An applicant who takes the middle road, avoids using extremes, and maintains vagueness in his answers will give the interviewer an easy justification for hiring him. The opposite is also true: If the interviewer does not like a candidate based on his first impression, he can justify his decision not to hire the candidate through selective hearing; by hearing the answers he or she wishes to hear. These types of interviews are not objective. Before conducting a job interview with an applicant, find out how objective you are by asking yourself if the applicant's answers will really matter. If you know nothing else about him or her, will you hire or not hire him based solely on his answers? If you cannot answer this question and keep your answer in mind throughout the interview, the interview will not be objective.

Objective questions must also be relevant. If the applicant gives you the answer you want, are you still certain that he would be a good candidate for the job? How do you know? Many answers fail to tell you much about a person's motivation or work ethics. Interviewers often ask about an applicant's background. But which is more important: asking what the applicant can do for the company, or simply verifying what he has already done? Why? Identifying what he has already done might demonstrate that he is trainable and hopefully has work ethics and vision. Selecting a good candidate for the job takes a willingness to challenge assumptions, even those coming from superiors, experts, or "reliable sources."

Thus rather than asking a candidate whether he or she is a team player, ask: "Tell me about a time when you applied the team player concept and the results of doing so." This will give you an idea of whether you and the candidate define "team play" the same. Many people also associate team play with outgoing personality and social skills. But what about the loner, the person who doesn't enjoy going to parties or only has few and select friends? The loner is often looked upon as someone who would not make a good leader. Is this necessarily true? Why or why not? If you ask an applicant to tell you about a time when he or she had difficulty solving a problem, and he says that he has never had such an experience, does this mean that he is smug and cocky, that he is lying, or that he is telling the truth and is in fact a very efficient leader?

GONE FISHING
(but not at the *Fish!* market in Seattle)

Now place yourself in the position of the team leader candidate. Once you are selected, you must know where you wish to take your team. If the interviewer asks what should be handled first: a message from an employee asking you to call him at home; a message from the manager asking you to report to him ASAP; or a situation where one of your employees has been injured on the job, what will you tell him? If you think about it, there really is not enough information to make a sound decision. The true answer to this question thus has to be a judgment call at the time it happens. To determine the urgency of the situation and make a sound decision, you must know, for example, if the employee injury in this hypothetical example happened right now or last week?

If the interviewer asks how you resolved a really difficult situation, what will you tell him? Remember that the term "difficult" is subjective, and what is difficult for one person may be easy for another. What if he asks you to define the term team leader? Although it might appear as though a good team leader wears many hats (leader, friend, problem solver, and role model), he works primarily in a support role to the team. Rather than dictating how the work should be done, you might want to suggest that he should solicit information from the employees to fully utilize his resources.

Team play involves the ability to work well with others, which involves breaking barriers between different teams and departments. But why do these barriers form? If you said "yes" to team play, describe a time when you applied the team play concept and broke some barriers. But don't stop here. Think the thought to conclusion and also describe the results. If, on the other hand, you had let the barriers stand, what would you have achieved? Or would it even have mattered whether or not you broke barriers? Without further clarification, the list of desirable leadership qualities is too weak to prove effective. Moreover, the image these leadership qualities paint in your mind most likely differs from the image they paint in somebody else's mind. For example, if a worker complains that the employees in a different department are lazy, and you say, "If you feel they've got it easier than you, then why don't you ask to work on their team next time?" how helpful do you think this reply is in breaking barriers? You have now become more about principle than about team play and will likely build barriers between yourself and your team rather than break them. A better way may be to ask why the laziness of the workers in the other department matters to your team. Once you understand where they are coming from, you can start forming a strategy for breaking the barrier.

Good leadership practices follow the model for learning: rote, understanding, application, correlation. **Rote** means that you can repeat back information by memory without understanding or being able to apply the information properly. **Understanding** means that you can explain the how and why of a situation but cannot necessarily perform proficiently. Although proficient performance comes with time and practice, proficient performance without understanding is mechanical and useless in a situation that requires adaptation. **Application** means that you can use the skill and perform tasks non-mechanically; it means that you can adapt by performing tasks under less than predictable circumstances. **Correlation** means that you can see how an issue *correlates* to another issue or to other material you have not yet learned. It means that you can use a skill intended for a specific task and apply it to another task without asking for help from others. All sources of information are valuable to the leader, but few are as valuable as those that help him or her use his knowledge to guide others.

Application = Give a man a fish and he will eat for a day.

Correlation = Teach a man to fish and he will eat for life.

Although specific techniques for performing a task can be taught, concepts are more difficult to teach. Intelligence is demonstrated through an understanding of the concepts and not through repetition of techniques, nor through the mindless repetition of popular slogans. Part of leadership thus encompasses mechanics of technique; the other part encompasses proper thinking. German philosopher Friedrich Nietzsche said, "What is great in man is that he is a bridge and not an end."[19] Next time you observe a member of your team using a different technique than the one called for when accomplishing a specific task, instead of correcting him, ask why. Then explain why or why not his technique has merit.

Intelligence is also the ability to carry a thought to conclusion, or in simpler terms, to see the full picture; to see how one issue correlates to another.

And yes, there are dumb questions and also dumb answers. But above all there are dumb people. When I asked supervision why we were working so short handed, they said, "Because management is not filling the open lines." Well, yes, thank you, that is obvious. So why was management not filling the open lines? The answer: "Because we are short handed." Obviously the leader who gave me this reasoning didn't know where he was going. Rather than walking in a circle, good leadership can be likened to a spiral staircase; you must be both in front of and behind your team at the same time. Lead from the front yet back them up not by walking in a circle, but by helping them climb closer to achieving the goal. This is also true regarding the reciprocal relationship between leader and team. If the leader stands behind the team's actions, the team will be more motivated to stand behind the leader's actions.

Now that we have an idea of the dangers of assumption and falling in lockstep with those who mouth popular slogans, let us examine in greater depth why using cheese, fish, and carrots as substitutes for real solutions to real problems can have disastrous consequences, and how to guard against the misuse, unintentional or otherwise, of popular slogans by management.

THOSE PESKY FOUR-LETTER WORDS

Motivational sayings are preached to us daily and posted on our walls, office doors, calendars, and day planners. But how many of these, "You manage things but lead people," have our leaders analyzed down to the component parts of the saying? How often have they actually done a *Jack and Jill* and asked the pertinent questions? How many of these sayings have really catapulted workers into great achievements rather than merely acted as a quick fix?

Years ago when a friend was going through a difficult divorce and suffered from stress and depression, his aunt said, "Chin up, today is the first day of the rest of your life!" Initially this sounded like something I might have said. But when he relayed the story to me I was ashamed, because he taught me that the ridiculous saying has no basis in reality. Not only did it utterly fail to explain what exciting new possibilities lay beyond this "first day of the rest of your life," it failed to state how he was supposed to go about achieving them. More importantly, he taught me that motivational sayings only work for those who are already motivated. Success through positive thinking has limits. Although a slogan may reinforce what you already believe, it will not help you make an about-face or feel better about an already bad situation. In other words, it is useless where real change or significant progress is needed. Consider the implications of the following statements:

1. There is always room for improvement.

2. Be proactive.

3. Be a team player.

4. Work smarter, not harder.

The idea that we can motivate people through euphemisms, or simply by assigning a positive meaning to a word, is disingenuous. Yet motivational books seldom question or explore to what extent we can fix a problem by changing somebody's attitude or assigning the problem a positive label. How often have you heard that there is always room for improvement; that set-backs are merely steppingstones to success; that failure is an opportunity for greatness; and the utterly untrue statement that what doesn't kill you makes you stronger? (Do you really think that a mother and father who lose their first child will really be psychologically stronger when expecting their second child? Do you really think that the thousands of soldiers who suffer from post traumatic stress disorder are really stronger thanks to their horrific experiences on the battlefield, simply because the war didn't kill them?)

The statement, "There is always room for improvement," is a cliché that leads us to believe that simply rewording a problem gives us an opportunity to improve. But there is a difference between coming up with new ways of doing our job and coming up with new ways that actually improve things and make our job more efficient. Unless we have analyzed and measured in some tangible way exactly what needs to be done and how it will improve the current situation, saying that there is always room for improvement becomes rather meaningless. Change does not automatically bring improvement and doing more (or doing something) is not necessarily a measure of success.

Consider the impact of "four-letter" words; you know, "don't" and "can't," which many motivational speakers, writers, and team leaders have said they would like to eliminate from our vocabulary. How many times have you been told that you should think positive and have a "can do" attitude? Yet the reason why the positive "do" has a greater impact than the negative "don't" is because of a principle of *learning*, and not because these words are inherently good and bad words that kindle or kill our motivation. It works like this: If you tell somebody to *do* something (such as, tell me your name, hand me that letter, etc.), his or her brain can immediately visualize what he is supposed to do. But if you tell him *not* to do something (such as, don't tell me your name, don't hand me that letter), his brain must first visualize what he is supposed to do (tell you his name, hand you the letter), before it can visualize what he is *not* supposed to do. This requires an extra step in the analytical process, which is why people seem to respond slower to the negative than the positive command. Let me demonstrate. Which of the following two statements has greater impact?

1. Be proactive!

2. Don't be reactive!

Number one has greater impact but not

because of the word "proactive," which is meaningless unless we assign it a meaning, but because of the sentence construction, which eliminates the extra step of having to visualize what one is supposed to be before one can visualize what one is not supposed to be. Now reverse it:

1. Be reactive!

2. Don't be proactive!

Which statement has greater impact? Which command is easier to visualize and follow? Still number one! Amazing, ain't it? Half-full is thus not inherently better than half-empty. Or as Sigmund Freud (1856-1939 CE) said, "Sometimes a cigar is just a cigar."[20] Real problems require real solutions, and whether the glass is half-full or half-empty is a matter of which direction the contents are flowing. If it is being filled, it is half-full; if it is being emptied, it is half-empty. If we don't know whether it is being filled or emptied, we don't have enough information to answer the question of whether it is half-full or half-empty. Simply assuming that a person who views the glass as half-empty has a negative attitude is insulting and demonstrates a lack of analytical capacity. Motivation comes through a desire to achieve something that has real value, and not through positive or negative commands.

Thus to determine whether something is good or bad, we must relate it to what we wish to achieve. Do is not inherently better than don't; can is not inherently better than can't; proactive is not inherently better than reactive; half-full is not inherently better than half-empty . . . Sunshine is not inherently better than rain. If we desire to get rid of what is in the glass, we would much rather view it as half-empty than half-full; if we have suffered a four-month drought, we would much rather have rain than sunshine. If we are going on a picnic, the reverse is true. Likewise, the four-letter words "don't" and "can't" do not automatically imply laziness, a bad attitude, or lack of confidence. After all, why should we all be overly zealous extroverts? Has it not also been said that silence is golden? Remember that your people could do a better job, *if* they wanted to. Your duty is not to make them do a better job, but to make them *want* to do a better job. *Want* is a four-letter word. When somebody says, "I can't do that," instead of saying, "Sure you can," or "You're so negative," ask, "What *can* you do?" or, "What do you *want* to do?"

Thus all four-letter words don't have the negative connotations of don't and can't. TEAM (Together Everybody Achieves More), for example, is a four-letter word and a popular one at that. Yet as previously mentioned, most people who mouth motivational slogans are simply repeating what they have read somewhere or heard at a motivational seminar they attended years ago. In short, they are using rote memorization without understanding. If I were to put you on the spot about the meaning of the TEAM acronym, my guess is that you would say something along the following lines: "You cannot place yourself ahead of the team, the team is more important than the individual, all for one and one for all, therefore, together everybody achieves more." But how do you know that what you just said is true and has merit? Besides, "all for one" sounds like communism to me.

To be effective, a leader must draw a following; he must know what is to be achieved and how to get there. The TEAM acronym fails on both counts. Together . . . how? Everybody . . . who? Achieves more . . . of what? As an employee, next time you go to work, pay attention to when sayings like these tend to appear, and you will likely find that it is not after great success has been reached that the leadership posts motivational bullshit on the walls, but rather when there are personnel issues they would rather not confront directly, such as impending cutbacks in salaries and personnel. When you already feel good about yesterday's accomplishments, the TEAM acronym may reinforce what you already know. But after weeks, months, or even years of obstacles seemingly without end, how effective is the same saying that motivated you yesteryear?

Furthermore, to speak the truth, we need to see things as they are and not as we wish them to be. Assigning a higher meaning to a word does not make it so. Using "displaced" rather than "bumped" does not make it hurt less when you lose your job. Or as martial arts expert Ed Parker (1940-1973 CE) reminded us: "[T]he spelling or pronunciation of the word designating self-defense does not add nor subtract from its effectiveness. In the case of the word 'punch,' in foreign language classes, it is spelled and pronounced differently. Yet, no matter what spelling or pronunciation it is given, it still hurts when it is delivered."[21] After taking a deep pay cut, how often have you heard people say, "Well, at least I've got a job"? Yes, it is better to be healthy and rich than sick and poor, as my grandfather used to say. But if you are sick and poor, it is better to acknowledge that you are sick and poor than pretend otherwise and fail to strive for a better future.

THE EMPTY SUIT

Although a job that presents opportunities for initiative and growth can enrich your life, as we have seen, a person who is not motivated by competition, or personal praise, or teamwork, or free tickets to a football game, will not respond to your grand plans. Everybody doesn't respond to the same type of motivation. If you want to use motivation to catapult your employees upward, you must also understand their passions, loves, goals, and desires. Furthermore, to inspire others, you must be watchful of certain motivation killers. For example, if you assign the most efficient employees the most difficult tasks or give them the heaviest workload simply because you know that the work will get done, you are in effect rewarding the slackers and punishing the good workers. Likewise, a certain motivation killer is asking an employee who finishes a task early to help other employees who constantly finish late, some of whom were most certainly wasting time.[22]

Now answer this question: There is a less than desirable job to be done, and you have two people who can do it. One is a star employee with a great deal of intelligence and great work ethics. You know that if you place him on the job, the job will get done. The other is a less talented employee, who often shows up late and does less than his share. In fact, he does barely enough to get by. What should you do? At one place of employment, this was a consistent problem. The best employees were doing the worst jobs, and over a period of months or years it wore them out. They were not happy anymore. Remember that an employee must feel good about working to be motivated. Yet when they asked the team leader why they were always placed in the worst positions, the answer was, "Because you're so good at it." Is this really the best strategy?

The reasoning may initially seem sound, because if you put the best people on the worst job, your stats will be met and your superiors will be happy. While if you put the worst people on the worst job, the reverse is true and you will have some explaining to do to higher ups. But what does this do to the attitudes of your best people? Perhaps a talented employee could excel even more if he were placed in a position that truly interested him? What about the less talented employee? Just how should the workload be divided? Should the most talented employee get the best job as a reward for being who he is? Should the less talented employee be punished with the worst job? If somebody performs poorly, should you train him so that he can perform better, or should you place him in another position that might interest him more? Do you build people's strengths, or do you try to eliminate their weaknesses? These are not easy questions to answer, but they matter and should be asked if you desire to gain insight into leadership. Finding a person's talents also requires that you are truly interested in finding his or her talents. In other words, you must care about him more than you care about your title.

An employee might prefer to work alone in a position where he can be the sole person responsible for organizing and planning the work. If this is his strength, would arguing that he is not a team player make him more efficient? If you really want to see a person shine, you must place him in a position where he can use his talents. No talent becomes evident until preparation and opportunity meet. Having the opportunity to use the talent is at least as important as having the talent itself. If the opportunity is not there, you will never know how talented the person is. How do you know what a person's talents are? Well, you can observe and make that determination over time. However, it might be easier to ask him or her directly. For example, you might see somebody type away at the computer at a hundred words a minute, and therefore feel that this person should be placed in a position that requires a lot of typing. But if he or she doesn't have the desire to work in the position you have in mind, you will do more harm than good by placing him there. The employee is the ultimate judge of what position is right for him or her. The best you can do is to question and guide.

The main obstacle to motivation is lack of desire. Others include:

1. Unfair treatment or critique. Fairness does not necessarily mean that everybody is treated exactly the same, and critique is not in itself an obstacle to motivation. In fact, it could be a catalyst, but the person critiqued must understand and agree with the critique.

2. Leader lack of interest, or appearing uninterested even if he or she is interested. If you have other things on your mind, you must still appear interested in front of your team or explain the reasons for your apparent lack of interest.

3. Physical discomfort or illness. A person who is sick or carries mental baggage must satisfy his personal needs first. A friend once told me, "If it ain't right at home, it ain't right at work either."

4. Apathy caused by inadequate preparation or inability to organize. Leader inability to take the efforts of the team seriously is a contributor to apathy.

5. Change. When change occurs, more than one person is affected. All those affected by the change must therefore know that their feelings are respected. Including your team in discussions for change can help alleviate this obstacle.

Motivational factors must also be challenging, achievable, and desirable. If the goals of the company and the goals of the individuals don't coincide, the goals cannot be used as motivators. Motivation also needs timing. The team must be ready to peak in order to peak. If the team lacks the necessary physical resources or carries significant mental baggage, you must choose a better time for presenting the motivating factor.

During a recent economic crisis, customer service at one company dwindled to the point that something had to be done to "teach" the workers the value of customer service. The company sent each employee to a one-day seminar that was a complete failure, because the employees' minds were not on customer service but on how to care for their families during pay cuts and layoffs. In fact, the employees were so angry that the seminar facilitator, a twenty-year employee of the company, was brought to tears.

This is called poor timing, and the results should have been anticipated. Just as we must satisfy our basic needs for food and shelter before we can satisfy our need for self-actualization, we must provide a solid base in the work environment before we can expect better performance. Before you can ask people to give, you must provide them with what they need: equipment, praise, opportunity, someone who cares. Once a person has these commodities, he will be more receptive to working hard and providing great customer service.

So let's say that you have managed to motivate the team to work efficiently, how do you preserve the hunger? Once motivation is achieved, it needs reinforcement and approval. A skillful leader can build enthusiasm by helping the individual perform successfully in front of his or her peers. Motivation also needs a concrete goal. Saying that "every day is a great day," or that you should "do something today that makes a customer smile," are weak motivators. Tangible goals, by contrast, heighten awareness and curiosity. Your team must also want to win. This may seem obvious, but if the team members can't care less whether they win or lose, not much will get done.

Rather than assuming that we all want to win, the question you should ask is this: What motivates the team to want to win? If winning doesn't come with a reward of some sort, if it carries no greater weight than losing, then why should the employees put forth the extra effort it takes to win? How do you define winning, anyway? Does everybody on the team agree with the definition? Tangible returns that are meaningful such as a bonus or an extra day off with pay, carry greater weight than intangible returns such as a "thank you" (although a "thank you" is nice, too, and is part of common courtesy). The moment you sense that you are losing the team, stop and remember that this is their career, too. Finally, as already emphasized, motivation needs ownership. This is why it matters who gets the credit. How do we know?

Let us visit the famous quote by American president Harry S. Truman: "It is amazing what you can accomplish, if you don't care who gets the credit." This sounds like a great quote. However, if your achievements are not acknowledged and you know in advance that they won't be acknowledged, how motivated will you be to put forth the effort? If you write a great book and somebody else is listed as the author, how much motivation will you have to write another great book? If you have studied the martial arts for twenty years but don't get to wear a black belt, even though others who have only studied for a year or two wear black belts, how motivated will you be to pursue your studies? Perhaps equally important, how helpful can you be to others when they don't know who you are or what you have accomplished? Getting credit for your achievements is absolutely necessary, because others are more likely to come to you for answers or advice when they know your background, knowledge, and achievements. When you graduate from college, do you not want a certificate to hang on your wall? Do you not want to be able to state your achievements on a job application to secure a better job or higher salary?

To get the most out of Harry S. Truman's

statement (or any statement or slogan for that matter), we must examine it within the context of our own times and circumstances. Remember that history does NOT repeat itself. Just because a particular statement was true for a particular person at a particular time, it is not true for all people at all times. "Need modifies law," said Swedish king Gustav Vasa (1496-1560 CE), "not only men's law, but occasionally God's law."[23]

Thus to serve its purpose, motivation must include more than empty words. By all means, set lofty goals that provide the desire to win, but don't present the team with an "empty suit." Speak the truth and identify the steps. Goals must be valuable to the individuals who make up the team, and my goals are not always your goals. How do you know that your goals or the proposed achievement has meaning to your team? You ask them. If your company's goal is "to become the world wide company of choice," and you are merely a lowly grunt, what specific images come to mind when you hear this goal stated, and why should you care? Why or why not does the goal motivate you? Exactly how does achieving the goal benefit you in particular? Most importantly, as the Greek critic and philosopher Aristotle (384-322 BCE) reminded us, goals must have duration and you must feel their impact every day: "For one swallow does not make a summer, nor does one fine day; and so too one day, or a short time, does not make a man blessed and happy."[24]

COSMIC CLAUSE VISION

Once the goals have been set, the vision must remain in view, because few people will find meaning in the journey alone without the promise or hope for something "better." If you feel as though you have been in the same ol' grind for twenty years, you probably have. A cosmic clause vision—a vision that is absolute or all encompassing in time and space, such as the "world's greatest"—is difficult to define and identify with and can therefore not serve as a great motivational factor. Being the greatest for the sake of being the greatest is meaningless. A better way is to state which specific part of the competition you need to beat and why. This creates purpose and gives your team a goal to work toward which, in turn, makes it easier to choose an appropriate course of action.

Furthermore, similarly to the problem with saying that "it is everybody's responsibility," because this makes it, in effect, nobody's responsibility because nobody will feel ownership, a vision statement must appeal to somebody in particular and not to everybody. Imagine trying to advertise this book as:

1. Equally good for leaders and followers of any company throughout the world.

2. Infinitely valuable to professional leaders, those coming up through the ranks, teams and employees, and everyday people alike.

3. Everything you ever needed to know and ever will need to know about any leadership situation at any time.

Which of the above statements did you choose? Which one gave you the greatest insight into what this book is really about? Which one made the book marketable? The answer is, probably none. Why? Because none of the statements appeals to anyone in particular. If you say that housekeeping is everybody's responsibility, do you really think that the break room at your company will be spotless at the end of the shift each day?

So what exactly is your vision? Whoever is first in line must know where we are going, right? And to end up where you want to go, you must know where you are right now. Moreover, not liking what you have but not knowing what you want makes navigation difficult. Many leaders have a theoretical understanding of what they want to achieve. The problems start when they have to translate theories into actions. Suppose that your company recently stated its vision in writing—To Become the World's Greatest—and printed pocket-size handouts for the employees as reminders. Is becoming the world's greatest a good vision? Obviously you cannot do much better than the world's greatest, so the vision certainly gives you something to strive toward. But on your road to becoming the greatest, where do you start?

Your vision will not be achievable unless you can state the goal in concrete terms and why it is important to achieve it. Your vision statement should tell you who you are and where you want to go. The vision, "to become the world's greatest," is weak because it fails to define who you are, who you need to defeat, and what you must do to reach your objective. In practical terms, it is as useful (or useless) as "to become a millionaire" or "to understand the meaning of life." If you do a *Jack and Jill* on the vision, you will no doubt achieve greater clarity. How do you define "greatest"? According to what criteria, and who is the judge? The world's greatest . . . In size? In service? In revenue? Next, who determines the size and scope of the "world"? Do you really need to serve every country on the globe to be the world's greatest, or is there some leeway here? What is the purpose of becoming the world's greatest, anyway? Why is it a worthwhile vision? Simply hanging inspirational posters on the wall and including a line or two in your vision statement about integrity and dazzling customer service does not make it so.

So let's try again, how good do we want to be? We want to be *very* good. Okay, so what? What does *very* mean? How about *very*, *very* good! Do you feel any smarter? I don't. Upon reaching the vision, we want our customers to be *very* happy. We also want our employees to be *very* happy. Very has a different meaning to different people. How rich do you want to be? I want to be *very* rich. Yeah, but . . . ? If your vision is to "nurture and encourage the (your company's name) culture," or to "find creative, new, and efficient ways of doing business," explain what the culture is and how to be creative. If your vision is to "be the biggest in the industry," or to "be the customer's number one choice," define biggest and explain what the customers want, and how you know that this is what they want. A problem with many motivational sayings is that nobody explains how to use them.

To prove meaningful, the vision must also be agreed upon and achievable within a reasonable timeframe. Think about this: Becoming the "world's greatest," is a vision that is not only difficult to define, it may not be attainable at all, at least not within the scope of the specific careers of your employees, so why should they care? How do you know that the vision is achievable? You know when you break it down into tangible steps. (Tangible = that which can be touched, felt, understood, and identified with.) It is better to present two or three definite steps than a list of twenty concepts. Rather than striving to become the greatest, you might want to state a slightly less valuable, yet more precise and achievable goal, knowing that it is a steppingstone toward the loftier vision.

Strategy is your plan and tactics are the particular steps you take or the means you use to realize your strategy. If you have a strategy but no tactics, your vision will remain on the drawing table; it will never be realized. If you have tactics but no strategy; your vision will become a trial and error type endeavor. Adhering to your strategy may mean the difference between success and failure. Or as they say in aviation: Plan your flight and fly your plan. Your strategy keeps you on track and helps you avoid stepping off the charted course. Your tactics take you step-by-step closer to reaching your goal.

Thus without a clearly defined goal and clearly defined steps, your vision, and thus your job, is nothing but a necessary evil that you partake in solely for the purpose of paying your bills. Few people will find meaning in the journey alone, with no promise or hope of a reward at the end of the tunnel. The same goes for your vision. If you cannot list the steps required, the vision will have little value. If the vision is not desirable, it will have little value. You must also have ownership of the vision; you must have reasonable control of the journey. The team must thus be updated on its progress. When evaluating how far you have come, be precise and avoid abstract words such as "we can" or "we know." Don't say, "We are way ahead of where we were this time last month." Give the team concrete evidence instead.

When you have defined the vision in concrete terms, continue by identifying the obstacles. Is this not negative thinking? Should we not state what we should and can do rather than talk about what stands in our way? "A chief of state does not want to hear a general in the field say that he 'hopes' to win tomorrow's battle or that he's 'visualizing victory'; he or she wants one whose plans include the possibility that things may go very badly, and fallback positions in case they do. Even that ultra-optimistic president Ronald Reagan invoked realism when dealing with the Soviets, constantly repeating the slogan 'Trust, but verify.'"[25] Remember that much of your motivation stems from the competition: Another's greatness can serve as a catalyst for your own.

Now consider what is wrong with these objectives and what barriers might stand in your way:

1. To make my team the best that it can be

2. To turn my company into a world-class champion

3. To make every customer smile

4. To build a company operated by people whose commitment ensures that customers will return for all of their future business needs

Now do a *Jack and Jill*: What does it take to be the best? If you are the best that you can be, is it enough to outdo the competition? Remember that you *must* win. How do you know where your limits are, anyway? What is meant by world-class? Is every customer really *every* customer, or just the majority? Why is it important that they smile? How do you achieve this? Without identifying the steps and the obstacles, the objective is meaningless. And being the best that you can be is meaningless if the competition is better.

One company recently issued a memo stating, "Each workgroup reviewed ranks near the top of the industry, and is projected to rank number two or three by the end of the year." Oh, did I tell you I just took second place? Good or bad? Taking second place is, in itself, neither good nor bad. We cannot make that determination unless we also know how many people were in the race. If it were just two, taking second place is not particularly admirable. If it were a thousand, taking second place is pretty darn good. Now do a *Jack and Jill*: What does it mean that each workgroup ranks number two or three if we don't also know how many contestants are in the race? When we cannot measure ourselves against tangible evidence, visualizing the next step becomes difficult.

The following sayings recently appeared on the walls at one workplace:

1. What have you done today that exceeded customer expectations?

2. Be proud. We are the world's greatest.

Let's look at number one first: Who is the judge? If you don't ask the customer what their expectations are, you have no way of knowing whether or not you have exceeded customer expectations. Now look at number two: Telling you that we are the world's greatest introduces an element of doubt; it implies that we are in fact *not* the world's greatest. If we were, we would have no need to say it. The natural development is to ask: Are we really the greatest? How do we know? And if not, then who is, and why? What constitutes great? Precision in definition is important if you want to present your employees with a roadmap that is void of confusion. You would be more successful if you said, "Our stock went up, the customers praised us publicly on national television, and you have a pay raise coming. Be proud. We are the world's greatest!"

Let's say that you reach your vision. Now what? What should you do once you get there? Is it enough to just barely become the greatest, or do you need to stay there and maintain a stronghold against the competition for time and eternity? And, if so, how? When setting goals or stating your vision, try to see what is beyond it. Your vision should not be the end result; it should be a steppingstone toward higher ground. If you ask "why" and "what next" before you get there, much of your journey will already be staked out. It will also help clarify if achieving the goal is going to cost you more than you are willing to pay, and if the achievement will be as valuable as you thought. It might make you more open toward considering other more profitable alternatives. Might there be times when it is prudent to cut your losses and run, to abandon the vision or objective for the sake of saving the company or the team? Or is it true that reaching the objective is not about feeling good but about getting it done? If you answered "yes," give an example. If you answered "no," know why. When taking the first step, as Prussian military strategist Carl von Clausewitz said, also think about what might be the last.[26]

NOTES

¹See Michael Pillsbury, *China Debates the Future Security Environment* (Washington D.C.: National Defense University Press, 2000), xxiii.

²Adolf Hitler, *Mein Kampf* (Boring, OR: CPA Book Publisher, first published in 1939), 38. Hitler also said, "Generally speaking, one should guard against considering the broad masses more stupid than they really are." Ibid., 105. Which of these two statements from *Mein Kampf* is correct? Which one would you use to support the views you hold? Hopefully you will see how easy it is to cherry-pick sentences as one sees fit from any larger account and find the idea or slogan one needs in support of one's views. The Bible might be the book that has been cherry-picked more than any other.

³Ibid., 43. To be fair it should be pointed out that there were German men and women who did not fall in lockstep with Hitler's ideals. A few voiced their opposition openly, but many more neither supported nor opposed the coming tragedy. However, as evidenced by numerous film clips and other documentation, the broad masses screamed with joy when Joseph Goebbels held his famous speech about total war in 1943.

⁴See Stephen C. Lundin, et al., *Fish! A Remarkable Way to Boost Morale and Improve Results* (New York, NY: Hyperion, 2000), 15-18 & 57.

⁵See Spencer Johnson and Kenneth Blanchard, *Who Moved My Cheese? An Amazing Way to Deal*

[6] with Change in Your Work and in Your Life* (New York, NY: Putnam & Sons, 1998), 21.

[6] See Barbara Ehrenreich, *Bright-Sided: How the Relentless Promotion of Positive Thinking Has Undermined America* (New York, NY: Metropolitan Books, 2009), 9.

[7] Ibid., 115.

[8] Ibid., 199.

[9] Marcus Buckingham and Curt Coffman, *First, Break All the Rules: What the World's Greatest Managers Do Differently* (New York, NY: Simon & Schuster, 1999), 141.

[10] See Wystan Hugh Auden, Wikiquote, http://en.wikiquote.org/wiki/W._H._Auden.

[11] Buckingham and Coffman, 133-134.

[12] Adrian Gostick and Chester Elton, *The Carrot Principle: How the Best Managers Use Recognition to Engage Their Employees, Retain Talent, and Drive Performance* (New York, NY: Free Press, 2007), 27 & 58.

[13] Ibid., 9.

[14] See John C. Maxwell, *The 21 Indispensible Qualities of a Leader: Becoming the Person Others Will Want to Follow* (Nashville, TN: Thomas Nelson, 2007), 4.

[15] Daniel H. Pink, "Big Bonuses Don't Mean Big Results," *Special to CNN* (Mar. 2, 2010).

[16] See Gostick and Elton, 87.

[17] Joseph Heller, *Catch-22* (New York, NY: Alfred A. Knopf, 2011), 56.

[18] The author is indebted to Professor Art Ritter at Westminster College in Salt Lake City for teaching how and why to ask the appropriate questions.

[19] Friedrich Nietzsche, Wikipedia, http://en.wikipedia.org/wiki/Friedrich_Nietzsche.

[20] Sigmund Freud, "Sigmund Freud Quotes," *Notable Quotes*, http://www.notable-quotes.com/f/freud_sigmund.html. There is some controversy as to whether or not this statement should actually be attributed to Sigmund Freud.

[21] Ed Parker, *Infinite Insights Into Kenpo: Mental Stimulation* (Los Angeles, CA: Delsby Publications,1982), 58.

[22] See Kitty Campbell, "Influence Employees the Right Way," *All Business* (May 1, 2002), http://www.allbusiness.com/human-resources/workforce-management/209349-1.html.

[23] See Franklin D. Scott, *Sweden: The Nation's History* (Carbondale, IL: Southern Illinois University Press, 1988), 65.

[24] Aristotle, Dictionary.com, Quotation by Aristotle, quotes.dictionary.com.

[25] Ehrenreich, 198.

[26] See Carl von Clausewitz, *On War*, edited and translated by Michael Howard and Peter Paret (Princeton, NJ: Princeton University Press, 1976), 584.

About the Author

Martina Sprague has a Master of Arts Degree in Military History from Norwich University in Vermont. As a historian she is particularly interested in political and social factors that influence the decisions of "Great Men" and the actions of their subordinates. She has written numerous books about military and political/social history. For more information, please visit her Web site: www.modernfighter.com.

www.ingramcontent.com/pod-product-compliance
Lightning Source LLC
Chambersburg PA
CBHW071619170526
45166CB00003B/1108